Paleo Cookbook for Beginners

---

50 Delicious Paleo Recipes for Beginners!

By: Natalie Ray

Disclaimer

The author of this book is not affiliated with any medical company, nor does the author provide medical treatment advice in any way. The ideas, views, and opinions expressed in this book are those of the author. The author assumes no liability for advice or suggestions offered in this book. The author and publisher of this book and the accompanying materials have used their best efforts in preparing this book. The author and publisher make no representation or warranties with respect to the accuracy, applicability, fitness, or completeness of the contents of this book. The information contained in this book is strictly for informational purposes. Therefore, if you wish to apply ideas contained in this book, you are taking full responsibility for your actions.

Paleo Cookbook for Beginners: 50 Delicious Recipes for Paleo Beginners! Copyright © 2013 by Natalie Ray. All rights reserved. No part of this book may be reproduced in any form without permission in writing from the author.

Table of Contents

Disclaimer 3
Introduction 8
Chapter 1 – Breakfast 10
- **Paleo Porridge** 10
- **Prosciutto & Baked Eggs** 12
- **Herbed Tomato & Bacon Frittata** 13
- **Carrot Banana Muffins** 15
- **Stir Fried Sausage Breakfast** 16
- **Blueberry Muffins** 16
- **Paleo Pancakes** 18
- **Fried Cassava Root** 20
- **Paleo Friendly Donuts** 22
- **Sweet Potato Hash** 24

Chapter 2 - Lunch 25
- **Guacamole Bacon Sandwich** 25
- **Shredded Fruit & Veggie Salad** 25
- **Liver and Onions** 27
- **Fish Sticks** 29
- **Chicken Wings** 30
- **Beef Stew** 32
- **Tuna Salad** 32

Salmon Cakes...34

Coconut Shrimp 34

Chapter 3 - Dinner..35

Prosciutto wrapped Asparagus 35

Turkey Meatballs 37

Chicken Fajitas..39

Paleo Meatloaf 40

Breaded Pork Chops....................................42

Teriyaki Chicken Paleo Style 42

Chili 44

Chicken Cacciatore......................................46

Taco Salad 48

Chicken Alfredo...50

Chapter 4 – Snacks 52

Apple Chips 52

Veggie Slices with Hummus Dip................54

Roasted Pumpkin Seeds 56

Mushroom Chips..56

Energy Bars 58

Zucchini Fritters 58

Chapter 5 – Smoothies...................................60

Chocolate Banana Shake 60

- **Mango Smoothie** 60
- **Caramel Paleo Milkshake** 62
- **Mixed Berry Smoothie** 62
- **Key Lime Smoothie** 64

Chapter 6 – Desserts 66
- **Chocolate Chip Cookies** 66
- **Coconut Paleo Popsicles** 67
- **Apple Paleo Pie** 67
- **Grilled Peaches** 68
- **Chocolate Mousse** 69
- **Stuffed Apples** 70
- **Paleo Custard** 71
- **Chocolate Cake** 72

Conclusion..73

Introduction

Congratulations! You are taking the first step towards creating a healthier you. Whether you have picked up this eBook as a way to lose weight or if you simply want to follow a healthier, more natural diet meant for humans, then you are on the right track. Would you like Paleo recipe ideas for your kids? My Paleo Cookbook for Kids provides with you 50 delicious recipes your kids will love!

The Paleo Diet, sometimes also referred to as the Caveman Diet, has proven it has many benefits to those that follow it. Not sure what Paleo really is? Cavemen lived during the Paleolithic time period, between 4500BC and 2000BC. The word Paleo is short for that time period when the cavemen lived and ate the foods that are now part of the Paleo Diet.

A Paleo Diet consists of foods that a caveman or woman would have eaten. In other words, if you couldn't hunt it or grow it and eat right away with little preparation, then it didn't get eaten. The Paleo Diet is a little more flexible now, simply because we don't have to cook over an open fire. But the foods that are consumed are still close to being the same foods.

Following are some easy to make recipes in the breakfast, lunch, dinner and snack categories. There are even a few smoothies and drinks that can be made that follow in to the Paleo Diet ideology. Once you have the basics down for the Paleo foods, then you can work your way in to more complex recipes to prepare.

For now, enjoy this beginner's guide to eating Paleo foods and feel yourself get healthy and fit each day you follow the diet.

Chapter 1 – Breakfast

Breakfast is the most important meal of the day. Your body is coming off of a short fast from the evening meal the night before and it needs to load up on protein for the coming day. It is important to pick protein rich foods that will fill you up and continue to keep your stomach full while you work and wait for the lunch hour to appear.

Following are some easy fixes for breakfast, when you are on the run to work or shuffling the kids off to their various practices for the day.

Paleo Porridge

Just imagine a cold, blustery morning outside your window, but a warm bowl of porridge in your hands. Suddenly, you have forgotten all about the weather and are focused on what is going in your tummy!

Ingredients:

2 cups coconut milk
2 bananas that are very ripe
¼ cup flax meal
¾ cup almond meal
½ tsp ginger
1/8 tsp cloves

1 tsp cinnamon
1/8 tsp nutmeg
Sea salt

Pour all of the ingredients in to a saucepan over low heat. Stir constantly and bring the mixture to a simmer. Stir for 3 to 4 minutes and pour in to a serving bowl. Sprinkle with maple syrup if desired.

Prosciutto & Baked Eggs

This tasty bit for breakfast can be made for an individual or it could be made for a group, using a large muffin tin. When baking for an individual, use one small baking dish.

Ingredients:

1 egg
1 slice of prosciutto
Salt, pepper & chives to taste

Whether using a baking cup or a muffin tin, wrap the piece of prosciutto around on the inside so it looks like a cup itself. Carefully crack the egg and pour the contents inside of the prosciutto. Sprinkle the seasonings over the top.

Bake at 375 degrees for 12 to 15 minutes or until the egg yolk is the level of hardness you desire.

Serve warm!

Herbed Tomato & Bacon Frittata

A frittata is an old school recipe, prepared for dozens of years by farm families with fresh eggs they brought in for the morning chores. Depending on how many you plan to feed, you can double this recipe.

Ingredients:

6 eggs
4 slices bacon
2 tomatoes, sliced
1/2 small onion, sliced
1/8 cup diced onion
1clove garlic, minced
1 tbsp basil
1 tbsp parsley
Salt and pepper to taste

In a large bowl, beat the eggs and garlic together. Stir in the basil, parsley and desired amount of salt and pepper. Set aside.

Cut the bacon in to strips and cook until crispy in an oven safe skillet. Save 1 tbsp of fat from the bacon. Add the diced onion to the pan with the remaining bacon grease and cook until softened. Add the garlic and bacon and cook until combined for 2 minutes.

Pour the egg mix in to the fry pan and reduce the heat to medium. Cook until the eggs have begun to set. Place the Layer the tomato and onion slices over the top. Bake at 350 degrees for 20 minutes. Remove and allow to sit for 10 minutes before slicing.

Carrot Banana Muffins

Do you have some bananas that need to be used up? Here's a great place to utilize them.

Ingredients:

3 eggs
3 bananas - very ripe
1 cup dates, pitted
¼ cup coconut oil
1 ½ cups shredded carrots
1 tsp apple cider vinegar
¾ chopped nuts
2 cups almond flour
1 tsp salt
2 tsp baking soda
1 tbsp cinnamon

Using a food processor, puree the eggs, bananas, dates, vinegar and oil until smooth.

In a bowl, mix the flour, soda, salt and cinnamon. Pour in the banana mixture and stir until combined. Add in the carrots and the nuts.

Scoop in to paper lined muffin tins. Bake for 25 minutes at 350 degrees or until a toothpick inserted in the center comes out clean.

Cool before serving.

Stir Fried Sausage Breakfast

This hearty breakfast mix will keep you filled up for hours.

Ingredients:

½ pound sausage, sliced
1 tsp coconut oil
½ small onion, diced
4 cups spinach

In a skillet, heat the coconut oil and add onions and cook until soft. Add the sausage pieces. Cook until the sausage is brown and stir frequently. Add the spinach leaves and cook just until wilted, about 5 minutes. Salt and pepper to taste and then serve.

Blueberry Muffins

These yummy muffins can be grabbed on the way out the door in the morning or even eaten as a snack between meals. These are so good you will forget it isn't the traditional way that grandma used to make them.

Ingredients:

½ cup tapioca flour

2 cup almond flour
½ tsp baking powder
½ tsp baking soda
3 eggs
1/3 cup honey
¼ cup coconut oil that has been melted
1 tsp vanilla
1 cup blueberries
Sea salt for taste

In a large bowl, mix the flours, powder and soda and set aside. In another mixing bowl, beat the eggs until they are fluffy. Add the honey, oil and vanilla and stir until combined. Combine the two bowls and mix until the dry ingredients have been absorbed. Pour in the blueberries and gently mix just until blended.

Scoop by tablespoon full in to a muffin tray sprayed or filled with liners. Bake at 325 degrees for 20 minutes or until a toothpick inserted in the center comes out clean.

Paleo Pancakes

Now it would seem like a pancake wouldn't be allowed in a Paleo diet, however, with the right flour it certainly is a Paleo friendly food. Coconut flour is used in this recipe making it gluten free, full of fiber and Paleo friendly.

Ingredients:

1 cup coconut milk
1 tsp vanilla
4 eggs
1 tbsp coconut sap
½ cup coconut flour
½ tsp sea salt
1 tsp baking soda
¼ tsp cinnamon

In a large bowl, beat the eggs and the milk until well mixed. Add in the sap and the vanilla and mix until combined. Add the flour, soda, cinnamon and salt and stir by hand just until the ingredients are mixed and the dry ingredients are absorbed.

Heat the griddle and let the batter sit. Once the griddle is hot, scoop ¼ cup or the desired amount on to the hot griddle. Cook until small bubbles appear in the top and then flip with a large spatula. Cook for an additional minute or two or until the bottom side is golden brown.

Serve the pancakes with other Paleo approved toppings such as honey, fruit or coconut nectar.

Fried Cassava Root

This recipe works in place of traditional hash browns that are made with potatoes.

Ingredients:

4 to 6 strips of bacon, cut up in to small pieces
1 medium cassava root
1 small onion
½ tsp ground sage
Salt and pepper to taste

Peel the cassava and then cut up in to bite sized pieces. Pour the cassava in to a saucepan and simmer for 4 minutes. Drain the water and set aside.

In a fry pan, cook the bacon until it is done. Remove from the pan and place on a plate covered in paper towels.

Using the same fry pan with the bacon grease, sauté the onions until they are soft. Add the cassava root in to the fry pan along with the sage. Stir and add the salt and the pepper to your taste. Continue to cook until the cassava is lightly browned, which will be about 10 to 12 minutes.

Pour in to a dish and serve warm.

Paleo Friendly Donuts

Don't think because you choose to follow a healthier diet that you also have to give up the favorite fall treats because you don't. Here is the homemade version of apple cider donuts that fall completely in line with the Paleo Diet.

Ingredients:

2 eggs
2 tbsp of liquefied coconut oil
½ cup apple cider – room temperature
½ cup coconut flour
½ tsp baking soda
½ tsp cinnamon
Dash sea salt

Topping:
½ cup coconut sugar
1 tbsp cinnamon

In a bowl, mix the flour, soda, cinnamon and salt and set aside.

In another bowl, beat the eggs until they are fluffy. Add the oil and honey and stir well. Pour in to the dry ingredients and stir until moistened.

Pour in the apple cider and stir by hand until the dough is combined.

Using a donut maker, scoop out the dough and place in to eat slot, according to the manufacturer's instructions. Close the lid and bake until done.

In a large plastic bag, mix the cinnamon and sugar.

Remove from the maker and immediately place in to the bag with the sugar mixture. Toss gently to coat. Serve warm.

Sweet Potato Hash

You don't have to totally give up potatoes to live a Paleo lifestyle; you can serve up some sweet potato hash at breakfast.

Ingredients:

3 large sweet potatoes, cleaned
2 tbsp olive oil
1 tbsp pepper sauce
½ tsp lemon pepper
½ tsp chili pepper flakes
½ tsp parsley
½ tsp onion powder
½ tsp garlic
½ tsp sesame seeds

Peel the potatoes and shred them over a cheese grater.

Mix in a large bowl with the seasonings. Heat the oil in a skillet and add the potatoes. Cook until the potatoes are tender. Serve hot.

Chapter 2 - Lunch

Lunch is a sometimes the meal done in a hurry, if you stay at home with the kids or have a busy day at work. But no matter what kind of day you have, you need to take time to have a Paleo friendly meal. This will keep you filled up until it is time to make dinner!

Guacamole Bacon Sandwich

Bacon makes everything taste better! Here is an easy bacon and guacamole sandwich to fix at lunchtime.

Ingredients:

4 strips bacon
Prepared guacamole
Romaine lettuce pieces – optional

Take one piece of cooked bacon and lay it on the plate. Spread a thin layer of guacamole over the top and then cover with lettuce if desired and another piece of bacon.

Shredded Fruit & Veggie Salad

This salad looks like a rainbow in your bowl when prepared.

Ingredients:

½ cup shredded red cabbage
½ cup broccoli florets
¼ cup shredded carrots
¼ cup diced green onion
1 tsp cilantro
½ tomato, diced
½ cup blueberries

Mix all of the ingredients together and then top with blueberries.

Liver and Onions

When you feel like a large lunch, vitamin rich liver is the way to go.

Ingredients:

5 onions, sliced thin
6 tbsp oil
Salt and pepper
4 slices beef liver

Add the oil to a skillet and heat. Once hot, add the onions and sauté until soft or about 20 minutes.

In another skillet, heat the liver and cook until it is done to desired wellness. Place on a plate and top with onions. Serve hot.

Paleo Pizza Bites

Sometimes you don't feel like a full pizza, so the recipe for pizza bites is perfect.

Ingredients:

Large pepperoni slices
Pizza
Sauce
Shredded cheese

Diced onion
Chopped mushrooms

Place the pepperoni on a baking sheet. Cover with a teaspoon of tomato sauce. Place the onion and mushroom over top and then add the cheese. Repeat for the remaining pepperoni slices.

Bake at 400 degrees for 6 to 8 minutes.

Fish Sticks

When the kids also share in a Paleo diet for you, it can be hard to find kid-friendly recipes. Here is one that both please adults and kids.

Ingredients:

1 pound of white fish bite sized pieces
1 cup almond flour
2 eggs
1 tsp sea salt
¼ cup grape seed oil
¼ cup olive oil

In a small dish, whisk the eggs and set aside. In another dish, mix the flour and the salt.

In a skillet, heat the oils.

Place the fish in the egg and then dip in to the flour mixture. Place in to the how skillet and cook until browned on both sides. Serve with ketchup.

Chicken Wings

Don't feel like going out? No problem, you can make chicken wings at home and feel like you are at the best restaurant getting an appetizer of your favorite wings.

Ingredients:

6 pounds of chicken wings
2 jalapeño peppers with the ribs and seeds discarded
½ small onion, diced
4 limes – wedged
3 cloves garlic – peeled
½ cup cilantro
¼ cup lime juice
Zest from lime
2 tbsp fish sauce
2 tbsp coconut aminos
2 tbsp coconut oil

In a blender, mix the onion, peppers, garlic, cilantro, lime juice, pepper, lime zest, coconut aminos and fish sauce. Mix until you have a smooth puree.

In a large, resealable plastic bag, add the chicken. (It might require two bags). Pour the puree over or split between the bags if you have two. Toss until all of the chicken pieces are coated.

Place in the refrigerator and marinate for 2 to 4 hours.

Remove from the fridge and allow to sit at room temperature for 30 minutes. Place on a hot grill and cook for 5 minutes on each side or until the chicken juices flow clear.

Beef Stew

Everyone has time for a bowl of stew on a cold fall afternoon, right?

<u>Ingredients</u>:

6 ounces beef stock
5 ounces red wine for cooking
4 cups canned tomatoes
1 pound stew meat
1 large onion, diced
2 medium carrots, diced
1 clove garlic, minced
1 tsp oregano
1 tsp basil

Brown the beef in the bottom of a stock pot. Add in the garlic, onion and beef stock. Simmer for 5 minutes. Add in the carrots and cook for an additional 5 minutes. Add in the tomatoes, wine, oregano and basil. Salt and pepper to taste. Simmer for at least 45 minutes before serving.

Tuna Salad

This is a light meal if you want to save yourself up for a big dinner.

<u>Ingredients</u>:

1 avocado – sliced
2 cans tuna, drained
2 green onions – diced
½ tsp red chili flakes
Juice from 2 lemons
Lettuce leaves

In a bowl, mix the tuna, onions, chili flakes and juice. Stir until combined. Serve over lettuce leaves and garnish with the avocado.

Salmon Cakes

For those of you who have access to good, fresh salmon, this is a delicious recipe to use for lunch or dinner.

Ingredients:

1 pound salmon fillet – skinned and deboned
2 tbsp coconut flour
½ tsp salt
2 eggs
¼ tsp white pepper
Coconut oil

In a small bowl, chop up the salmon so it is in fine pieces.

In another bowl, mix the eggs with the flour, salt and pepper. Add the salmon and stir until completely coated.

In a skillet, heat the oil. Scoop the salmon mix by teaspoons and place in the skillet. Flatten with a spoon. Cook on each side until it is golden brown.

Coconut Shrimp

When you have a hankering for seafood, here's a delicious coconut shrimp recipe to try.

Ingredients:

1 can coconut milk
1 pound raw shrimp in shells
1 tsp ginger root, peeled and minced
1 clove garlic, minced
¼ tsp pepper
¼ tsp salt

Wash the shrimp but keep them in their shells. Cook them in a saucepan with the milk, garlic, ginger salt and pepper over medium heat. Bring the mix to a boil and simmer for 15 minutes over low heat.

Peel the shells and serve warm.

Chapter 3 - Dinner

It's time for dinner! This meal is where you can enjoy your food after a long day and start working on the menu for the next day! Make sure that all of your dinners include a healthy salad and some side dishes to keep you filled up.

Prosciutto wrapped Asparagus

This recipe can work for an appetizer, side with your dinner or whenever you feel the urge for something delicious.

Ingredients:

Slices of prosciutto
Slices of asparagus, cleaned

Take one piece of prosciutto and 1 asparagus spear. Start at the bottom of the stalk and wrap the prosciutto upwards.

Place a dollop of desired oil in the bottom of a skillet. Add wrapped spears in and cook for 4 minutes or until desired crispiness has reached. Serve warm.

Turkey Meatballs

Do you feel like a twist with your meatballs? How about making them out of turkey and vegetables?

Ingredients:

1 pound ground turkey
2 carrots, diced
5 large mushrooms
½ small onion
1 green pepper
1 clove garlic
2 tsp garlic salt
2 tbsp Italian seasoning
Salt and pepper to taste
Parsley

In a food processor, combine the carrots, pepper, onion, garlic and mushrooms and pulse until chopped. Pour in to a bowl and mix well the seasonings until combined. Stir in the turkey by hand and mix until all ingredients are combined. Salt and pepper to taste.

Form in to 1" balls and place on a cookie sheet. Bake at 350 degrees for 20 to 25 minutes. Serve warm or place with BBQ sauce.

Chicken Fajitas

How about a touch of Mexico with dinner tonight?

<u>Ingredients</u>:

1 pound boneless, skinless chicken breasts cut in to strips
1 tbsp coconut oil
3 cloves garlic
1 tsp chili powder
1 tsp cumin
1 tsp oregano
½ red onion – sliced
2 red bell peppers – sliced
2 heads butter lettuce
Juice from one lime and 1 lemon

In a small bowl, combine the oregano, chili powder, cumin and garlic. Roll the chicken pieces through and then place in a hot skillet with the coconut oil. Add the onions and cook for 4 minutes. Stir often until the chicken pieces are almost done. Add the peppers and juices. Stir until the ingredients are combined. Serve over the lettuce.

Paleo Meatloaf

This is a Paleo version of traditional meatloaf.

Ingredients:

1 ½ pounds lean ground beef
1 egg
2 tbsp coconut milk
1 small onion, diced
1 cup chopped red cabbage
4 minced cloves of garlic
1/3 cup almond meal
1 tsp garlic powder
1 tsp chili powder
1 tsp ground mustard
½ tsp ground pepper
¼ tsp sage

Add the egg, onion, milk and cabbage in a large bowl and combine. Add in the remaining spices and stir well. Scoop in the beef and mix by hand until all of the ingredients are combined.

Press in to a greased loaf pan.

Bake for one hour and 20 minutes at 350 degrees. Allow to set for 5 minutes before slicing. Serve with BBQ sauce or ketchup.

Breaded Pork Chops

These breaded pork chops have a bit of zing to them.

Ingredients:

4 pork chops
1 ½ cups almond flour
2 tsp cayenne pepper
3 tbsp coconut oil

In a small bowl, mix 2 tbsp of oil and the pepper. Roll each pork chop in to the mixture and then in to the dish of almond flour to coat.

In a skillet, heat the remaining oil. Add in the pork chops and cook for 5 to 8 minutes on each side or until meat is cooked through.

Teriyaki Chicken Paleo Style

How about a little Asian inspired meal for dinner tonight?

Ingredients:

1 pound of boneless, skinless chicken breasts
1 tbsp coconut oil
1 small onion, diced
1 cup pineapple pieces

1 medium red pepper, diced
3 romaine hearts
¼ tsp sea salt
¼ tsp black pepper
Coconut aminos

Cut the chicken in to bite sized pieces and place in to a hot skillet with the coconut oil. Add the onions and cook until they are slightly soft. Add in the aminos and cook for five minutes. Add the pineapple, pepper, salt and pepper and stir. Cook through until the vegetables are tender. Serve over the romaine.

Chili

A hot bowl of chili can be served any time of the year, but cold and wintry days are the best! This recipe can be made for lunch or dinner, any time.

Ingredients:

2 pounds lean, ground hamburger
2 tbsp coconut oil
56 oz canned tomatoes
8 oz green chilies
1 onion, diced
2 carrots, peeled and diced
1 zucchini, diced
2 tbsp chili powder
1 tsp cumin
1 tsp garlic salt
1 bay leaf
½ tsp thyme
½ tsp oregano
1 red pepper, diced

In a large pot, add the oil and the hamburger. Cook the hamburger until it is no longer pink. Pour in the remaining ingredients and bring to a simmer. Allow to cook for one hour on low, stirring frequently. Garnish with parsley to serve.

Chicken Cacciatore

This is another Paleo friendly dish that is a healthier version of the traditional recipe.

Ingredients:

3 pounds of chicken pieces
3 tbsp coconut oil
1 small onion, sliced
1 green pepper cut in to pieces
½ pound of mushrooms, cleaned and sliced
Salt and pepper to taste
1 can diced tomatoes
1 can tomato sauce
3 cloves garlic
1 tsp oregano

In a skillet, heat the oil and add the chicken. Brown the chicken on all sides and then remove from the pan to a plate.

Using the same pan, add the onions and mushrooms and cook until they are soft. Add the rest of the ingredients and stir well. Add the chicken and then salt and pepper to taste.

Bring the mix to a boil and simmer over medium low heat for thirty minutes.

Taco Salad

When you want some Mexican and don't know what to make, look to a salad to keep you full.

Ingredients:

1 pound lean ground beef
1 small onion, diced
2 tbsp chili powder
1 tsp garlic salt
½ tsp sea salt
½ tsp oregano
1 small jar salsa
¾ cup water

Toppings
1 medium tomato, diced
3 romaine hearts
1 avocado

Brown the beef in a skillet until it is no longer pink. Add the onion and cook until it is soft. Stir in the remaining ingredients and bring to a simmer.

Scoop out over the romaine and then garnish with tomato, avocado pieces and olives if desired.

Chicken Alfredo

You can still have your pasta, just a bit differently.

<u>Ingredients</u>:

1 pound boneless, skinless chicken breasts cubed
2 tsp olive oil
4 minced garlic cloves
1 cup cashews
2 tsp tarragon
½ tsp onion powder
¼ tsp pepper
¼ tsp garlic powder
¼ tsp ground mustard
1/8 tsp paprika
Sea salt to taste

In a skillet, heat the oil and then add the garlic. Sauté until soft and then add the chicken pieces until browned. Remove chicken.

Rinse the noodles and place in to the hot skillet. Add the tarragon and simmer for 30 minutes.

Drain the liquid and reserve for the sauce.

In a blender, add the cashews and seasonings and grind until a fine powder. Add the reserved juice and pulse carefully.

Return the sauce to the skillet and mix well with the noodles. Cook for an additional 10 minutes.

Chapter 4 – Snacks

Sometimes your breakfast or your lunch just didn't fill you up or you have a while until it is dinner, so you are reaching for a snack. There are lots of yummy snacks to prepare that are friendly to Paleo dieters.

Apple Chips

Instead of grabbing a bag of potato chips, these apple chips are much healthier and tastier, too.

Ingredients:

2 large apples for baking
2 cups apple juice
1 cinnamon stick
1 tsp cinnamon

In a saucepan, heat the juice and the cinnamon stick until it boils.

Cut the top and the bottom of the apple and then make very thin, approximately 1/8" thick slices. Drop each slice in to the boiling mixture and boil for 5 minutes.

Remove the slices on to a wire rack to cool. Sprinkle with cinnamon and then place the entire rack on a cookie sheet. Bake for 30 minutes at 250 degrees. Remove, cool and then serve.

Veggie Slices with Hummus Dip

The hummus dip can easily be packaged up with veggies for a snack to eat anywhere on the go.

Ingredients:

Carrot sticks
Pepper sticks

1 head cauliflower – cut in to small florets
2 tbsp olive oil
3 cloves garlic
½ cup tahini
Juice from 1 lemon
2 tsp cumin
1/8 tsp paprika
1/8 tsp black pepper

In a bowl, mix the cauliflower, oil and cumin together. Dust with sea salt if desired. Pour in to a baking sheet and bake at 500 degrees for 25 minutes. Stir one to two times to keep the mixture from browning too fast.

In a food processor, mix the tahini, garlic and lemon juice until smooth. Add the cooked cauliflower mixture. Blend until it reaches your desired smoothness. Serve with carrots and peppers or you choice of veggies.

Roasted Pumpkin Seeds

Do you like a little crunch with your snack? Pumpkin seeds ought to do the trick.

Ingredients:

Pumpkin seeds
Sea salt
1 tsp olive oil

Clean the seeds and place in to a large pot of water and 1 tsp sea salt. Boil for 10 minutes. Drain the seeds and spread out over paper towels to dry.

Spread the seeds on a baking sheet. Drizzle the oil over top and then stir the seeds carefully to coat. Sprinkle lightly with sea salt.

Bake at 325 degrees for 10 minutes. Remove from the oven and stir, and then cook for an additional 10 minutes.

Allow to cool on the tray and then remove to a large container. Serve cold.

Mushroom Chips

This super simple recipe only requires two ingredients, shitake mushrooms and sea salt.

Ingredients:

Cleaned and stemmed shitake mushrooms

1 tsp sea salt

Place the mushrooms with the top down on a baking sheet. Sprinkle with sea salt. Bake at 300 degrees for 20 minutes. Allow to cool before eating. Mushrooms will absorb moisture in the air quickly, so store in an air tight container or eat them before they go soft.

Energy Bars

These energy bars make a great snack, but they could also work for a breakfast on the go.

Ingredients:

1 cup mixed dried fruit
1 cup pitted dates
1 cup roasted almonds

Mix the ingredients in a food processor and pulse to break them up. Stir if it becomes big clumps and then pulse again. Once they are small pieces, continue to pulse for 1 minute.

Remove from the processor and press in to a greased 8" pan. Store in the refrigerator overnight. Cut in to bars in the morning and keep covered until serving.

Zucchini Fritters

When you plant zucchini in the garden, you will always be looking for recipes that taste good and use it up!

Ingredients:

3 eggs

2 medium zucchini, shredded with the skin on
1 tbsp coconut flour
½ tsp sea salt
¼ tsp pepper
Coconut oil

In a bowl, beat the eggs and slowly add the flour to it. Add in the zucchini, salt and pepper and stir until combined.

In a skillet, heat some coconut oil. Drop zucchini mixture in by the teaspoon and allow to cook until golden brown. Serve warm.

Chapter 5 – Smoothies

Smoothies and shakes are a great way to satisfy your sweet tooth and fill up your stomach. There might be sweetness in the recipes, but all contain foods that are allowed in the Paleo Diet!

Chocolate Banana Shake

This recipe is sweet enough you will think you died and went to heaven.

Ingredients:

½ to ¾ cup of ice
1 banana
½ cup coconut milk
1 tbsp honey
2 tbsp cocoa powder
Dash of vanilla

Add all of the ingredients in to a blender and cover. Puree until they are smooth. Pour in to a tall glass and serve with a straw.

Mango Smoothie

This might not look like a mango smoothie because it is green, but it is!

Ingredients:

1 peeled and diced kiwi
2 cups kale – branches and stems cut off
1 peeled and diced mango
Juice from ½ lime
1 cup coconut milk

In a blender, pulse the mango and the kale leaves. Add in the kiwi, lime juice and milk and blend until smooth. Pour in a cup and serve cold.

Caramel Paleo Milkshake

Do you have a sweet tooth? Here's a drink that is sweet yet Paleo friendly.

Ingredients:

1/3 to ½ ripe banana
2 pitted dates
½ cup almond milk
1 tsp maple syrup
1 ½ tsp cashew butter
Ice cubes
Dash salt

In a blender, pulse the ice cubes. Add in the banana and dates and pulse again. Pour in the remaining ingredients and blend until smooth. Pour in to a cup to serve.

Mixed Berry Smoothie

Enjoy the fruits from summer and blend them in to a fresh smoothie.

Ingredients:

½ cup blackberries
½ cup raspberries
½ cup blueberries
Ice
1 cup coconut milk
1 tsp fruit spread

In a blender, pulse the ice. Add the berries and pulse again. Pour in the milk and fruit spread and combine until smooth.

Key Lime Smoothie

Feel like you are in the tropics, no matter where you live!

Ingredients:

Juice from 4 key limes
1 cup coconut milk
1 banana – ripe
1 tsp lime zest
1 pitted date
¼ tsp vanilla
2 cups spinach
Ice cubes
1 tbsp sunflower butter

In a blender, pulse the ice. Add the remaining ingredients and blend until smooth. Pour in to a glass to serve.

Green Smoothie

When people see green smoothie, they usually run away in fear. But this recipe is delicious and one you will want to make over and over.

Ingredients:

6 romaine lettuce leaves
4 large kale leaves with ribs removed
1 ½ cups coconut water

3 stalks celery
½ cup coconut milk
½ orange – peeled
2 tbsp flax seed – ground
½ apple, seeded and chopped
Juice from one lemon

In a blender, pulse the romaine and kale leaves. Add the remaining ingredients and puree until smooth. Pour in to a cup and serve cold.

Chapter 6 – Desserts

Being on a diet doesn't mean that you have to suffer or go without. There are plenty of Paleo friendly recipes that can be served as a dessert after a meal. While these dishes might be a healthier version of desserts you used to consume, you should still eat them in moderation to keep your calorie count in check!

Chocolate Chip Cookies

This is great as a snack for the kids after school or to send off to school as a treat. Or whenever you just feel like a cookie.

Ingredients:

1 tbsp vanilla
½ cup melted coconut oil
½ cup maple syrup
¾ cup dark chocolate chips
2 cups coconut flour
2 cups almond flour
½ tsp baking soda
½ tsp sea salt

In a bowl, mix the flours, salt and soda and set aside.

In another bowl, mix the oil, vanilla and syrup. Stir in the dry ingredients. Pour in the chocolate chips and stir just until combined.

Scoop by the teaspoon and drop on to a cookie sheet. Flatten with the back of the spoon. Bake for 8 minutes at 350 degrees or until the cookie is golden brown.

Coconut Paleo Popsicles

This sweet treat is great for a hot day.

Ingredients:

1 can coconut milk
1 tbsp honey
½ cup grilled pineapple chunks

In a bowl, mix all of the ingredients. Pour in to popsicle molds and freeze until firm.

Apple Paleo Pie

This is a take on the traditional apple pie recipe – but just a bit sweeter.

Ingredients:

Crust

1 tbsp carob powder
1 ½ cups sunflower seeds
¾ cup raisins

Place all the ingredients in a food processor and grind up until smooth and sticky. Fork in to the bottom of a 9" pie pan. Set aside.

Pie

¾ cup honey
6 baking apples, cored, peeled and diced
1 tbsp cinnamon
¼ cup shredded coconut
1/8 tsp cloves
Juice from ½ lemon

In a large bowl, mix the apples, lemon juice, honey, cloves and cinnamon until the apples are all covered. Pour in to the pie crust and flatten with a spatula. Sprinkle the coconut on the top.

Place in the refrigerator for at least one hour to set. Cut in to slices and serve cold.

Grilled Peaches

This is a yummy dessert to add to the grill once your meal is over.

Ingredients:

2 peaches - cleaned
¼ cup coconut oil
1 tsp honey

Half the peaches and leave the skin on. Dip the cut sides in to the oil and then place on a hot grill. Cook for five minutes and then flip over. Once the peaches are flipped, drizzle with honey and grill for another few minutes until the peaches are soft.

Chocolate Mousse

How about a cold treat on a hot day? You can make your ice cream and eat it too.

Ingredients:

1 can coconut milk – chilled overnight
2 tbsp cocoa powder
2 tbsp sunflower seed butter
1 tbsp maple syrup
1 tsp vanilla
1 tbsp honey
Shredded coconut
Dark chocolate chips

Place all of the ingredients in a food processor except for the coconut and chocolate chips. Puree until smooth and fluffy. Pour in to a serving dish and then garnish with the chocolate chips and the coconut.

Stuffed Apples

Fall is a great time to use apples, a great sweet fruit that is Paleo friendly.

Ingredients:

2 apples, cored
½ cup almond butter
½ cup almonds

Place the apples in a baking dish, already cored.

In a bowl, mix the butter and almonds. Spoon half in to the center of each apple. Bake at 300 degrees for 15 to 20 minutes or until the apple has become soft. Serve warm.

Paleo Custard

Sometimes you just might have a hankering for something smooth. How about some custard?

Ingredients:

1 can coconut milk
1 vanilla bean
3 eggs
2 ½ tbsp honey
2 bay leaves

In a bowl, whisk the eggs.

Cut the vanilla bean down the center and place in a saucepan with the milk and bay leaves. Heat only until it is close to simmering.

Take one ladle of hot milk out of saucepan and stir it in with the eggs. Pour the entire mixture back in to the saucepan and cook until thick, about 5 minutes.

Remove from the heat. Discard the bay leaves. Scrape the inside of the vanilla beans and stir in to the mix and throw out the pods. Stir n the honey and pour in to an 8" baking dish. Cool before serving.

Chocolate Cake

Got room for cake?

<u>Ingredients</u>:

1 ripe banana
3 eggs
10 pitted dates
2 tsp vanilla
½ cup coconut oil
½ cup cocoa powder
½ cup coconut flour
1 tsp baking soda
¼ tsp salt

In a food processor or blender, add the dates and pulse slowly. Add in the banana and mix until a puree has formed.

Pour in to a large mixing bowl and add the eggs and vanilla and stir well. Add the coconut oil and stir. Slowly add in the flour, powder and soda. Mix until the batter is smooth.

Pour in to a greased 8" pan. Bake for 30 minutes at 350 degrees or until edges are set.

Cool completely before slicing.

Conclusion

These recipes prove that you can take a traditional recipe and change it up just a little bit to make it fall in to acceptable options when following a Paleo lifestyle. These recipes are pretty basic for the most part and made with ingredients you will be stocking in your pantry since you are converting in to or already following a Paleo diet.

Once you have mastered the basics, then you can move on to more complicated recipes and experiment with fussier ingredients. But until then, work on the basics and getting used to a different way of cooking, shopping and eating, because it is a bit of a transition for most people. Don't be ashamed if you can't fully convert over to a Paleo diet right away. For some people, they need to gradually use up items in their pantry and start buying items that are Paleo friendly and not just go cold turkey on to it. Start with baby steps if you have to, but always keep working towards incorporating more and more Paleo friendly recipes in to your diet.

Good luck and remember that your changes are getting a healthier, fitter and in the long run, happier you.